The Diary of
A 100 Year Old
Amused Senior

Estelle Craig

authorHOUSE®

AuthorHouse™
1663 Liberty Drive
Bloomington, IN 47403
www.authorhouse.com
Phone: 1 (800) 839-8640

Published by AuthorHouse   03/11/2015

ISBN: 978-1-4969-7454-9 (sc)
ISBN: 978-1-4969-7453-2 (e)

Library of Congress Control Number: 2015903648

Print information available on the last page.

This book is printed on acid-free paper.

Introduction

When I decided to write this book, I had a problem. My eyesight had diminished to the point where I could no longer read a newspaper or even a book. I certainly could not sit at the computer because I could not see what was on the screen, or use the keyboard. My daughter, Robin, suggested that I use the microphone in my iPad. My assistant, Cristina, would transfer it to my email. We would then transfer my email to Robin's email, and she would transfer this to her husband, Robert, who would transfer it into his computer. He would send it to my daughter Sheri, who would proceed to edit it. Robin also did the cover design, and took the photo.

So it took a committee of four people plus me as writer to make this book possible. I want to thank Sheri, Robin, Robert and Cristina for their help and devotion.

I

This is the diary of an amused senior.

I am 100 years old and I can't seem to see any wrinkles on my face. That's because I take my glasses off when I look in the mirror.

I am an amused senior. I am fortunate in so far as I can walk erectly, talk, and think. I am amused by things that happen each day. Some days I seem to see better than other days. Some days I hear better than I do other days. Changes seem to happen every day so I have to be alert. Can I make it from the bed to the bathroom and back to bed? Well, that's great!

I had a friend who told me this little story. She was driving her car in Florida, and needed to find I-95, the busy interstate highway. She could not find it. She was lost. She was just driving around and saw a man sitting in front of his house. She pulled her car up to him and asked, "Do you know how I get to 95?" He said, "Sure. Eat healthy foods and drive carefully." He should have added, "And keep your mind active." And that's one way to get to 95.

I am amused because I am able to converse with people who are impressed by my memory and the fact that I'm aware of current events. I remember my name and their names. I am able to carry on fairly intelligent conversation with one or more people, and I still feel that there is much more for me to do in this world. I have travelled frequently for long distances and would like to resume travelling. However, I cannot rely on my legs taking me too far. But I still have my memories.

Until two years ago, I was able to live alone, shop, cook, do many things for myself that I am not able to do today. Fortunately, Cristina came into my life. Now I don't have to worry that there is something I need to do and need help doing it. And I can go to bed at night knowing that if I need help, there is someone here to help me.

People seem to feel that I have done something special by approaching my hundredth birthday. They seem in awe of it. But I think more and more people will be living longer from now on if they live healthy lives. I do think it's important to keep busy, to keep your mind open, to read, and do things now that you're older that you didn't have time to do when you were young. Most of my long-time friends have departed this world, but I am fortunate that I have a caring family who visit me as often as each one can. Sometimes I relive my childhood days and regret some of the things I did, and some of the things I did not do. Other days I'm glad that I did some of the things I did. My motto is "Yesterday is history, tomorrow is a mystery, and today is the present." So enjoy it.

When I was busy growing up in New York City, and I was in my teens, I took for granted some of the various activities that were available to me. Some of them were free, some of them a very low cost. Of course, this was during the Great Depression and very few people had any money.

My friend Henry and I would take a double-decker bus, which had an open top. We would climb the steps to the top of the bus and try to get seats up front. The bus would go down Riverside Drive, along the Hudson River, turn on to Broadway and continue its drive down to Greenwich Village. That trip was 10 cents and took almost an hour each way. If you stayed on the bus you did not have to pay any more money for the return trip. It was a lovely way to spend the evening.

Henry and I would sometimes play tennis on the site where the George Washington Bridge now stands. There was no charge for that and we enjoyed many hours of playing there. We also visited art galleries and museums where sometimes entrance was free, and if there was a charge, it was minimal. Times Square was a great place to walk around at night. Lights were everywhere. We found Grey's drug store, which had a counter where they sold last-minute theater tickets. For less than $2 you could buy a seat for a Broadway show. If you waited until 15 or 20 minutes before show time, the price would drop even lower.

Going to the theater in those days was a magical event. When the house lights were lowered just before the curtain parted, there was a hush in the audience that I will never forget. Today, although we still have excellent theater, it is not the same.

Since I am now a senior inching her way toward her 100th birthday I am not able to go to the theater as often as I would like. But I am very fortunate to be living in an age that has produced such devices as iPads, audio tapes, Kindles, computers and CD players. They keep me busy all day.

Sometimes when I have difficulty falling asleep, my memory starts recycling the things that happened to me so many years ago. I can recall quite vividly an afternoon in New York City when a friend and I went for a walk along the shores of the Hudson River. We had climbed down the cliff and were walking along when we noticed a gang of boys coming in our direction. We did not like the fact that we were two girls, 14 years old, with the gang following us, and we thought we had better get back to the top of the cliff.

So we started to climb up before the boys could reach us. Halfway up my friend, Frances, and I froze. We couldn't move up and we couldn't move down. We simply couldn't move. The boys were starting up after us. Fortunately for us there were some people at the top of the cliff and they saw our predicament. One of them came down and helped us climb up. Frances and I never took that walk again.

One of my favorite recollections is going to the theater to see vaudeville. There were three theaters not too far from where I lived, and one of them had a vaudeville show every weekend. I loved to sit up front in the theater and watch the acts. Generally there were four or five acts and very often the show featured a headliner. I would look at the dancers and observe their costumes, their make-up, and very often I could see runs in their mesh stockings. I saw the Ritz Brothers, who were very big at that time, and many other headliners. It was fascinating to watch the shows, followed by a feature-length picture.

I don't recall exactly how much I paid to enter the theater, but it couldn't have been more than 50 cents, or I would not have been able to afford it. Other movie houses showed double features, plus the news, plus a travelogue, plus coming features, and some of them also gave away dishes after you paid for your tickets. The Depression was at its height and people counted their pennies before they spent some on unnecessary things.

In those days all the films were black and white. There was no sound track. The very first time I heard sound in a movie was the sound of horses' hooves. Today, of course, it's unusual to see a film that is not in color, and, of course, we take sound for granted. There has been a great change in the film business.

Occasionally I find myself thinking of my mother. She was one of seven sisters and one brother. The oldest sister lived in Detroit. The others lived in New York City. Where the brother lived no one knew. No one ever spoke of him. I never knew his name. I never knew what he had done to make his family angry with him. It is still a mystery to me.

My mother and father were married in New York. They moved immediately back to his home in Massachusetts. Eighteen months later they had a little girl who was born two months earlier than was expected. She was a seven-month old baby. Almost six years later I was born in Waltham, Massachusetts.

My mother was very unhappy living away from her sisters. At some point she must have convinced my father to move back to New York City, although he had his own business and was doing well. So they sold their home and moved back to New York. The plan was to go into business with my Uncle David. But it didn't work out, so he opened a jewelry store in Manhattan. I was probably five or six years old at that point so I don't remember too much of that move. But my mother was very happy to be reunited with her sisters.

And so began Sunday meetings at their parents' home, with all the sisters sitting together in one room and the husbands in another room. I was put together with my cousins in another room. Because I was just a few years older, I became their leader, but actually I wanted to be with the adults. I loved hearing their gossip.

My mother was the second oldest sister. They were all two or three years apart in age. The next oldest, Lisa was two years younger than my mother. She told everyone that she was going to be rich someday. And she did become quite wealthy when she married a man who had a very successful business. Next in line was Molly who was very high spirited and had red hair. The other sisters all had dark hair and they teased Molly, that she really wasn't their sister. Molly and her husband had a small business together. Unfortunately her husband died in a car accident. Molly carried on with a little help from Lisa.

Next in line was Sarah. I was told in later years that Sarah was the most beautiful of all the sisters. She had been courted by a man she didn't much like. She kept telling him she wouldn't marry him. But as her other sisters were all getting married she finally decided to marry him. He owned a building in Manhattan where he ran a business in a store downstairs, and they lived in an apartment upstairs. But Sarah wasn't happy in that apartment. She wanted a house, a large house, which they couldn't afford in Manhattan.

So she found one in the country. When her husband closed his store for the night, he had to take the subway and then a bus in order to reach their home.

By this time it was late at night and Sarah was usually in bed when he arrived home. He had the money from his day's sales and he would sit at the edge of the bed and cover Sarah with the money. However, the marriage did not last very long even though they had two children. Sarah dabbled in real estate, and if her husband was down and out, she would let him sleep in her basement.

The second youngest sister, Fanny, was the one I liked the best. I could talk to her as I could not talk to my mother. I felt that she was my friend. She married a man who loved music. They had one son. I don't remember what her husband did for a living but I do know that during the Depression he lost his job and was forced to work for Lisa's husband, David.

My youngest aunt, Anne, was a puzzle. In those days women married quite young. She didn't marry until she was almost thirty. She was very intelligent and quite bossy. She earned a good salary. She rode a horse in Central Park. She traveled a lot. Sometimes she would bring me back souvenirs from her trips.

In later years she and her husband visited me in Toronto. After entering my house and saying hello, she looked around my living room, which was quite large, and started to move my furniture without permission. I did not like her arrangements, but I knew she would be gone the next day so I let it stay the way it was until she left.

She had one son and found it difficult to raise him. Years later her son told me that when he was seven or eight years of age, she had given him some kind of cereal for his breakfast and he didn't really like it. She told him that he had to sit there until he finished it. He sat for a long time before he noticed that the window was open. It was winter and there was snow on the ground below. He took the horrible cereal and dumped the contents of his plate out of the window. Then he called his mother and told her he was finished eating. The next morning she took a plate of cereal from the refrigerator and placed it in front of him. She had seen him dump the cereal out of the window the day before, and had scraped it off the snow. This time she sat with him and he was forced to eat it.

Unfortunately, she died some years later, and her husband remarried. He seemed to be very happy with his second wife, and told me that there was nothing better than a second marriage. His new wife had a daughter from her previous marriage. The girl was in her late teens and came to live with them. She went on their honeymoon with them. She went everywhere with them. A few years later my uncle became ill and had to be hospitalized. He thought he would be going home when he recovered, but instead his wife put him in a nursing home. He was lonely there and unhappy. He died soon after. So much for a second marriage!

A young child does not see his or her parents. My mother was just my mother. I know she had long hair which was pinned into a bun. She was neither slim nor fat. She told me that she weighed 98 pounds when she was first married. One day she announced that she was going to have her hair cut off into a bob. That was a big step for her. She wore a corset with bones in it, and she sighed with relief when she took it off at night. She never used makeup as I can remember.

I recall her telling me one day that she was blessed because she enjoyed doing whatever she had to do. Whether it was a household chore, or helping my father in the store, she was happy to do it. I was busy playing with my friends. We played jacks, stoop ball and various other games. One game consisted of kicking an object, whether it was a bit of pottery or tin, along a diagram which we drew with chalk on the sidewalk.

One day while we visited the home of one of my aunts, I noticed in a glass cabinet a lovely set of china. One of the cups in the cabinet appealed to me, so I opened the cabinet door, took out the cup, and threw it on the floor and broke it. I think I was seven at that time. Of course it was a terrible thing to do, but I was forgiven for it.

I was raised under my mother's mantra, "Children should be seen but not heard." I was told that many times, and it did affect my life. We did not have much of a family life together. The store came first. Sunday was the only day we all had dinner together. My father had an insurance policy which called for two people to be in the store at all times when it was open. Hours for retail stores at that time were brutal. They were open from 9 in the morning until 9 at night. So if my father wanted his dinner, my mother had to be down in the store. The watchmaker would be the second person present.

Years later when I was around fifteen, I remember being in the store with my father. There was a courtyard behind with a huge window above the watchmaker's desk, and huge shutters. My father had climbed up to close the window, but not the shutters as yet. Suddenly we saw a man in the courtyard looking into our window. He had a large handkerchief tied around his face and wore a cap pulled down over his face. He motioned with his gun, waving it up and down.

My father spotted him and shouted at me to get down behind the counter because I was in a direct line of the gun. Then my father ran out on to the street, calling for help. I was still crouched down. I thought how glad I was that my father had closed the window only 10 minutes before this happened.

I became a teenager very early in life. I entered high school when I was eleven. Most of the other students were thirteen or fourteen. So it was difficult for me to be around the older students who were certainly more mature than I was. Most of the girls wore lipstick and many of them wore shoes with heels. I was not allowed to use lipstick, so I bought a tube out of my allowance and put on the lipstick when I got to school. This was a whole new world to me. Most of us had "slam" books in which we posted remarks about other people in our class. Some of us got crushes, the girls on boys and boys on girls.

My family did not hold birthday parties very often, but when my sister reached her sixteenth birthday, my parents gave her a splendid party. All the aunts, uncles and cousins came. She received many gifts, but the one I liked best was a quilted bathrobe. It was a peach color made of satin, and I thought it was the most beautiful robe I had ever seen. I wanted one just like it but I was only ten then, and I knew I had to wait until I was sixteen to get one. But a few years later, the Depression started. And quilted satin bathrobes became a thing of the past.

When I turned sixteen there was no talk of any party, nor did I expect one. That morning my mother asked me to deliver a piece of jewelry to my aunt Lisa, who lived in Brooklyn. My aunt had asked my father to have it repaired and she needed it. So off I went on the subway for the long ride to Brooklyn. Aunt Lisa had three children, the oldest close to my age. They wanted me to stay and play with them, which I did. In the late afternoon, I thought I had better start for home, but the children begged me to stay. My aunt, who knew something I didn't know, did not encourage them. She told me to call my mother and ask if I could stay later. My mother told me she wanted me to come home.

So I left and took the subway back home. It had been a tiring trip and I thought it would be good to get back. When I got home and opened the door there was a crowd of people singing Happy Birthday to me. I was in my old clothes and I was tired after playing with my cousins and taking the long subway ride. I was in no mood for a birthday party. My mother had arranged to get me out of the house by sending me to deliver the jewelry to my aunt. I was grateful to my mother and sister for organizing the party, but I would have liked to look better and not feel so tired.

I know I could have done a lot better in high school than I did. However my grades were good enough to get me into Hunter College, which gave free tuition. I thought I wanted to be a lawyer. At that time there were very few female lawyers and that seemed attractive to me. The courses that I chose were all wrong for me, and in my second year I decided that I would go to school at night and try to find a job in the day time.

II

There were very few jobs available then. So many people were unemployed. I scanned the newspapers and saw an ad for people to sell typewriters. So I decided to see what that was all about. The address was in the Daily News building. The room was full of people. I was seventeen at that time.

As I was standing there, two young men came over to me and one of them said that his friend wanted to meet me and be properly introduced. So he introduced me to his friend, who would become my future husband. His name was Louis David Craig. He lived in Brooklyn with his family and today was his birthday. He had just turned twenty-two. He had spotted me across the crowded room, and said he just had to meet me.

Just then there was an announcement that the meeting was about to begin. We found seats and a man began to speak. He told us that the company was selling Royal portable typewriters.

They were sponsoring a radio program featuring a man called Cowboy Tom, who would sing cowboy songs and talk about the splendors of owning a typewriter. The typewriters would be sold for five dollars down and 10 cents a day. Tom would ask people to send in for information and in this way he would collect the leads that we would be given, and then we would go to see the people who had written in and try to sell them a typewriter.

Some of the people in the room got up and left. They were not interested. But Louis and I thought we would give it a try, since we both wanted to earn some money and had no other jobs. We agreed that we would meet the next day to get the leads we needed to sell typewriters. The next day I met him at the office and as we waited for the meeting to start someone sat down at the piano and began to play "Home On The Range". We began to laugh, and joined in the singing. Then we were given our leads and a typewriter and told to try hard to sell them.

I sold two typewriters that day, one to each of two of my aunts. They each paid the full amount. They certainly would not bother to pay ten cents a day, and they did it to help me out.

The next day when I reported I had sold two typewriters I was cheered, and had to make a little speech. I was happy to have made 10 dollars. We were given new leads, and we had to sing "Home On The Range".

Louis asked me to go out with him on Saturday night and on our second date he gave me his fraternity pin. He said we were engaged. He never proposed. He just took it for granted that we would marry when he got a good job. He had graduated from Cooper Union as a chemical engineer, and had no luck in finding a job in his field. We met every day for coffee. He would write me little poems. I would reply with a poem of my own. We would sit for hours before returning to our homes. And then a miracle happened. He got a job in his field. It did not pay very much, but at least he had a weekly salary and did not have to sell typewriters anymore.

Now that Louis had saved a little money, he decided to take me out in style. We both dressed up in our best clothes and went down to the restaurant that Jack Dempsey owned. He was a famous heavyweight champion boxer who was known all over the world. When we arrived, he was standing in the doorway of his restaurant and shook our hands as we entered. We were seated at a nice table and given menus.

We were startled to see the prices, they were very high. We didn't know what to do, but decided that since we were there we might as well order something. So we ordered hamburgers priced at 75 cents, the cheapest things on the menu. Normally you could buy hamburgers at that time for no more than 25 cents. But we had a grand time and could boast of eating at Jack Dempsey's and even having shaken his hand.

I was tired of selling typewriters too, so I quit and got a job in my uncle's factory. It wasn't a good job, but I made 11 dollars a week, working six and a half days a week. Louis, who lived a long way from me, would take the subway on a Saturday evening. It was more than an hour's ride from his home in Brooklyn, to my apartment in upper Manhattan. We would go out for the evening, then he would take me home and then he took the subway back to his home. It was a long night for him and as time went on, I got permission from my mother to let him sleep over at our apartment.

One day he saw an ad seeking a chemical engineer for a job in Buffalo. He went up for an interview and was hired. He was told he would earn 27 dollars a week. He was excited, and told me we would now be able to get married. He did not know that the chemical engineers in this company had gone on strike, and the company was trying to hire young graduate students to fill the places of the strikers.

My parents did not want me to get married before my sister did. She was not dating, and I did not see why my life had to hinge on hers. Louis was now living at the YMCA in Buffalo. He wrote to me every day, and expected me to do the same. He asked me to arrange a wedding date, and take care of all the wedding arrangements.

We had set up a dual bank account containing 86 dollars. I decided to buy myself a trousseau, so I withdrew the money and bought myself a navy blue going-away suit and a hat to match. I also bought a gorgeous long red gown with a deep low cut open back. It had long sleeves, and I fell in love with it. With the remaining money I bought a long black velvet gown with frilly chiffon sleeves. I don't know where I thought I might wear these gowns, and I realized it was a foolish thing to do, but I had to have them.

Before Louis went to Buffalo he made me promise that I would visit his family at least once every two weeks. Since they lived at one end of Brooklyn and I lived at the other end of Manhattan, it was a long subway ride, and so I had to stay overnight at his home.

When he first introduced me to his family, his mother told him not to marry me because I was too skinny. However that didn't stop Louis. When he went to Buffalo I kept my promise that I would visit his family. There really was not much room for me there. The family lived in the flat downstairs in a two-story duplex. Louis had two sisters and one brother. His brother was 10 years younger than he was and the two boys shared one bedroom. His parents had the other bedroom. There were only two bedrooms in that flat. His two sisters shared a pullout couch in the living room. But when I came to visit and had to sleep over, there was no room for me. I had to share the pullout couch with the girls, and that meant that I had to sleep in the crack in the middle of the couch. That was not very comfortable.

Finally it was time for the wedding. Louis had bought A car for 75 dollars. He drove to Manhattan and packed a rented tuxedo and his best pair of shoes, which were brown. When he arrived he was extremely tired and went right to sleep. The following day he went to his parents' home to prepare for the wedding.

I did not have to shop for a wedding gown. Both of his sisters were models. The older of the two girls was married in June, and our wedding was set for the end of August. She was kind enough to lend me her wedding gown. It was a simple white satin dress with long sleeves and came with a long veil. I think She may have paid 20 dollars for the gown.

On my wedding day I dressed at home and one of my uncles volunteered to drive us to the hotel where the wedding ceremony was to take place. Since it was a very hot day, I decided not to wear any hose. It was a small wedding. I had not been permitted to invite any friends. There was no music available, but the hotel had arranged for the wedding song to be piped in by Muzak for the beginning of the ceremony. There was no music at the end. When the ceremony was over Louis led me to the elevator to get to the room provided for us by the hotel. At the door he swept me into his arms and carried me into the room. Then the phone rang. I answered and someone said, "Mrs. Craig." "I'm sorry," I said, "she's not here." I did not realize the fact that I was now Mrs. Craig. It was like a scene out of "Gone With The Wind." But "Gone With The Wind" had not yet been written.

The next day we left for Buffalo. No wonder I am an amused senior. When I think of that ride up to Buffalo, I still laugh, but I didn't then. The car that Louis had purchased for 75 dollars had her own personality. I like to give my possessions names, so I called her Elizabeth. Elizabeth thought it was her honeymoon.

We had no money or time for a honeymoon. When Louis left Buffalo for the wedding, he had asked his boss for a week off, without pay, of course. The boss said no, but Louis took the week off anyway. He had been so lonely in Buffalo without me. The car was very slow, but the distance between Manhattan and Buffalo is not that great. However it took five days for us to get there.

The year was 1934 and there were no highways such as we have today, so we drove through little towns. There were no motels then, there were no Holiday Inns, there were only houses with rooms to rent. There were a few hotels, of course but we could not afford to stay at them. All we wanted to do was to go to sleep after a long day with Elizabeth.

One of my aunts had given me a lovely lingerie set. It was made of the purest silk and so beautifully stitched together. It consisted of a long nightgown, a slip, and panties. Slips at that time were worn by almost every female, so that your body would not show under your dress. It seemed a pity to wear that elegant nightgown in those dingy houses.

Anyway we were driving and Elizabeth was whining saying, "Water, water, I need some water." Louis didn't even seem to know that I was in the car, that we had just been married, that I was a new bride.

His focus was on Elizabeth. "Come on honey, we can do it." Sometimes she did, sometimes she didn't. So we spent our nights in those very little rented rooms and we finally arrived in Buffalo.

Louis led me very proudly into the furnished apartment he had rented for us. It was dreadful. The furniture was old and broken down. The rooms were dark. There were three entrance doors which had to be checked every night before going to sleep. The place looked so dreary to me but at least we had arrived. I pulled out the bed linen, made up the bed, and we fell asleep, thoroughly exhausted.

The next morning Louis left for work. He was told that because he had taken the week off to get married he was now to be on the midnight shift, working from midnight to 8 a.m. So that night he left for work at about 11 o'clock and I got into bed. I was quite lonely and I was not happy about this arrangement. The fog horn sounded all through the night. If it was windy, the doors would rattle and there were three of them. I was not sure whether it was the wind or someone was trying to get in.

It was about nine in the morning when Louis came back. I was already out of bed and I prepared a meal for him. Then he got into bed and slept until late afternoon. We had a few hours together, I gave him some dinner and packed a lunch for him and he went off to work. Then I got back into bed. It was a busy bed. But I had not expected it to be this way.

I decided to look for another apartment, but before I could do this we had a call from Louis' mother telling us that she was coming for a visit. We really had no room for her and we had not invited her. She was a difficult woman who did not seem to like anyone. She never invited anyone into her home, not even her husband's brother and his family. She didn't seem to have any friends. I tried to be polite. She told me she saw how we slept. I'm not sure I knew what she meant by that.

After she left, I started to look for another apartment. I found a much nicer place for 40 dollars a month, the same amount of money we were already paying. Things started to look better for us. Louis was put on another shift, from four in the afternoon until midnight. I found a friend. She was the wife of a man Louis was working with. I liked her and it made my life so much better to have someone to talk to.

We were in Buffalo for almost six months when Louis was fired. The strikers were back at work and the services of their replacements were no longer needed. I don't think I was ever so happy in my life when I learned that Louis was fired. Buffalo is a very nice city, but in the winter it is very cold. The fog horn made sad music all night long. It was very depressing. We put our things into Elizabeth's trunk and started back to New York City. We had no place to stay in Manhattan but my parents were good enough to let us stay with them until we could find quarters for ourselves.

At this point, Louis had no job. I had no job. But I had an idea. I knew he was a good chemist and I persuaded him to develop a formula for a nail polish remover in cream form. Nail polish removers always come in liquid form. Sometimes the bottle leaks, or spills over. That liquid nail polish remover can cause a lot of damage if it is packed in a suitcase and spills. It can cause damage if placed on a table and falls over. I felt by making it into a cream form it would eliminate that kind of damage. So Louis devised a formula and we made it at night in his father's workplace where he manufactured dolls.

There was sawdust all over the floor, a fire hazard as far as the formula went. We bought a large coffee maker in which the formula was made. I had created a label, which I thought was attractive. It was gold and the lettering was black. We called the product Craigette. The rest was up to me to put labels on the jars and then sell them. I found the names of buyers for the large department stores in New York and I went to see them so I could sell Craigette.

They seemed to like the product but there was a problem. It didn't seem to work. I solved that by putting nail polish on my nails just before I went in to see the buyers. So the polish was still a little wet. Craigette now easily removed the polish. I sold it quite easily and Macy's and other department stores included it in their ads.

Louis found a better job and we decided to sell Craigette. We found a buyer, and I found a job at the New York Herald Tribune. Of course, I had to deny that I was married or I would not have been hired.

Almost a year later, Louis saw an ad for a company seeking a chemical engineer experienced in paint. That is what he had been working on. This company was in West Virginia. He set up an appointment, went to West Virginia, and was hired. Both Louis and I thought it was a great adventure, but my parents were very unhappy.

We decided to replace Elizabeth with a new car that we could really trust. We named him Caesar and we headed for Huntington, West Virginia. It is a trip of 750 miles, and Caesar knew what he had to do. He did it passing gas stations without crying for water.

When we arrived in Huntington we checked into the hotel and the next day Louis reported for work. I started looking for a place for us to live. We felt we could live a reasonably normal life now.

III

Since I was a married lady now of 21 or 22 I knew that I could not work so I decided to go back to college to try to get my degree. Midterm my mother called me and asked me to come back to New York because she needed me to solve a problem that she had. The train trip was 17 hours each way. Of course, I took the next train. Most people were not flying as yet, and Huntington did not have a proper airport.

Huntington was the largest city in the state of West Virginia and then had a population of 85,000 people. I reflected on the difference between living in New York City with its crowds of people, tall buildings and fast pace of life. I compared this to the style of living in Huntington. There were very few tall buildings, very few apartment buildings because most people preferred to live in houses there. So that if you wanted to live in an apartment it was probably going to be in a duplex or a triplex. I found an apartment in a duplex and we sent for our furniture which had been placed in storage in New York. I was so taken with the difference in the style of living in Huntington as compared with crowded New York that I decided to write an article about this. I sent it in to a top magazine, which was published in West Virginia, and it was accepted and published in the next issue. I was paid with six copies of the magazine.

Louis came home for lunch every day so I had to prepare three meals a day. If I needed help with my housekeeping, I could always hire someone to help me. The going rate for a cleaning woman was 25 cents an hour. I had time to do other things. I joined Community Players and acted in several plays. I also auditioned for a radio program that produced plays. I was accepted, and acted in some of the productions they put on.

We had two major newspapers in Huntington, a morning paper, The Huntington Herald Dispatch, and an evening paper. They were both owned by the same company. I preferred the morning paper, but saw that there was nothing much of interest for women in the paper, just news and sports. So I decided to go down to speak to the editor of the Herald Dispatch. I told him that I would like to write a little column that might interest women. He knew that I was married and he told me to go home and take care of my husband. I said that I could do that and still write the column. He finally told me to write something, so that he could judge if I really could write. I went home and wrote a small article and brought it back to him. He liked it and told me I could try to write a column and then we would see whether it would be successful.

So I wrote a column and he printed it. My name was at the top of the column, which was called the Women's Exchange, because I did want to exchange ideas with other women. People seem to like it and started writing in to me. The column grew in size. In a short while, my picture was put at the top of the column.

Now I had a problem because nothing very much happened in Huntington, so I had to create news. I had never been to a prizefight, so I went to one and wrote about it from a woman's point of view. I went to various events. I even went to jail to see how they treated women. I wrote about anything and everything that I thought would interest women. And they seemed to be interested in what I wrote, because they wrote letters to me and I printed some of them. I had a good thing going. Not very much, of course, but I enjoyed doing it and trying to do your thing is what will interest people.

While the decade of the 1930s was not the greatest in the world and there were some awful things going on during the Depression, the decade ended with the great World's Fair. People came from all over the world to visit the World's Fair, which was held in Flushing Meadows outside Manhattan. I was still writing my column and when I told my editor that I was going to New York to visit the fair, he gave me a press card. I took my parents with me to the fair.

Of course, we wanted to see the main display that was attracting so many people, the General Motors Highway of the Future. There were lines of people waiting to get in. There were hundreds and hundreds of people in the lines but when I produced my press card the General Motors people made me a member of the General Motors Press Club. They stopped the lines and let my parents and me get in without waiting, We took the seats assigned to us. Then the seats began to move on the tracks and we travelled along the Highway of the Future.

It seemed incredible then, in 1939, to see the highways that we take for granted today. People couldn't imagine then that we would ever have roads like that. But then people couldn't imagine that we would ever have the traffic that we have today. I was pleased that I was able to take my parents to this great display and have them get in without waiting, especially since they didn't go out very often together.

After living in Huntington for two or three years, we had saved a little money. We decided to buy a house. We found a small one and paid 1,200 dollars for it. The taxes were 27 dollars a year. After we moved into the house, we seemed to have much more space. One day when I was in the downtown district, I passed a furniture store and I noticed a piano inside the window. It was beautiful. I had missed playing the piano, so I went into the store. The piano was a Baldwin, and was built like a grand piano. The Baldwin name was equal to that of Steinway.

One of my wedding presents was a saxophone. I tried to play it, but the reed hurt my mouth so I put it away. I decided to tell the salesman about the saxophone, and asked if I could trade it for the piano. Now the piano was very modern looking, and we had modern looking furniture. Most of the people in Huntington did not have modern furniture, so they were not interested in a modern looking piano. It would not fit into their homes. After a huddle we agreed on a deal. For 100 dollars and the saxophone I got the piano.

It was the early '40s and it was early May. It was Kentucky Derby time. The weather was great and we set out for Louisville, Kentucky where the Derby was held.

In those days women of all ages, young and old, never went out without a hat, so I pulled out my best hat to wear for the trip. It was a stove-type style with a maroon ribbon above the brim. I thought I looked very elegant.

On the way we stopped at the Mammoth Caves and decided to go in. There were places where we could stand erect and other places where we had to get down and crawl on our hands and knees. There I was wearing my elegant hat, crawling through those tiny spaces, crawling with my hat atop my head, just barely making it through.

We finally left the caves and headed for the Derby. It was a glorious day. We arrived in time for the second race. Neither of us was experienced in horse racing and betting. I decided to bet a few dollars on the uniforms the jockeys wore. Or maybe I would put my money on the looks of a horse. I bet 2 dollars, sometimes 5 dollars. We sat through the next four races, and decided we had had enough. So we left. We did not know that the Derby was the seventh race. We left before the real Derby was run. So we attended the Kentucky Derby without really being at the main race.

We were very hungry at this point and tried to find a place to eat. We finally wound up at a farm house where they served us the most delicious chicken dinner I have ever had. The gravy that came with the chicken was so good that I asked for the recipe. I have used it ever since and I tell everyone it is an old family recipe going back many years. We started for home and when we got there found that someone had broken into our house and robbed us. We did not have very much taken from us, since we did not have very much. It had been a very interesting weekend, and I still have that hat.

Louis and I had now been married for almost seven years and had not even thought about our future, or of having children. It suddenly dawned on me that this might be the time to start a family. So we did. I felt very sick for the first few months, and stopped writing the column. I felt too sick to write.

One day when I was in my seventh month I woke up and said to Louis, "I don't want to live here anymore." He looked at me as though I had gone crazy. "Why? We have a good life here." I told him that I didn't want to have a child in West Virginia. I wanted my children to live where they had relatives, where they had grandparents. We had no one there. Yes, we had friends, but it wasn't the same.

Louis gave his company two weeks' notice. We put our house up for sale and sold it quickly for 1,400 dollars. We put our furniture in storage until we knew where we would be living in New York. We had bought a dog and wanted to take him back with us. We called him Barry. When Louis, Barry and I got into the car for the long trip back to New York I was very happy to be leaving Huntington and have a chance to be with my family again.

IV

The year was 1942 and Louis' job was with the Office of Price Administration. I had found a very good doctor not far from my parents' apartment. I knew what hospital he worked with so I was set for the birth of my child. But Louis told me that he would have to work in Washington, D. C. That was a blow. I had found an apartment that I liked, but I had to let it go. My mother suggested that I stay with her until the baby was born and then I could go to Washington, but I did not like that idea. If Louis had to live in Washington then I would live in Washington.

So in my seventh month I packed my things and took the train to Washington. It was war time. It was difficult to find a place to live. Louis grabbed a newspaper as soon as it came off the press to see if he could find a place where we could live. He found some houses that the government was putting up for people like us who were working for the government. But they would not be ready until six weeks before the baby was to be born. Before we could get into the house, he found a sublet for the two weeks where we would stay until we moved into the house.

I dip into my memory box now and I recall when we moved into the place. It was terribly hot in Washington. The apartment we had sublet had no air conditioning. Barry and I would climb the two flights the back way up to the apartment because we were not supposed to have any pets in that building. Louis and I would go to the movies some nights to cool off. When it was time to move into the house, I felt good. Barry and I were busy in the house, everything was put away and I went about my duties without any problem.

The due date had just arrived and I was busy hanging curtains in the living room. We had had no phone since it was difficult to get a phone in those days. But Louis had somehow managed to get one. I remember that I was on a ladder hanging curtains when the doorbell rang. I got down from the ladder and opened the door. It was the postman with something I had to sign for. As the door was slightly open, Barry, who did not like the postman, ran out and ran down the street. I ran down the street chasing him, caught him and went back to the house.

I climbed the ladder again and the phone rang. My first phone call. It was Louis. He wanted to know how I felt. I said I felt fine except that I felt a little tickle in my back. He hung up and called my doctor. Then he called me back and said, "Get your bag. We're going to the hospital." I had a bag packed so I was ready to go. We got to the hospital, and my daughter Sheri was born one hour later.

We lived in Washington for one year, and then Louis went to work for the Manhattan Project. That means that he was working on the atomic bomb project. Now we went back to New York and I had to find a place for us to live.

We stayed at my parents' apartment until I could find an apartment for us. And it turned out to be a nice little place in a complex where there was a playground in a park. There was even a supermarket nearby and a Macy's department store in that same complex.

Now I know I am a great believer in destiny. I have had many instances in my life, as I look back over the years, when things that have happened affected my life. For example, one evening Louis came back from work and said, "I think I just saw Gilbert driving by as I was looking for a space to park my car." Gilbert was a man who had gone to the same school as Louis, Cooper Union. He was a year ahead. He was also the man Louis had worked with in Buffalo and it was his wife who became my friend. Unfortunately, she had died and we lost complete touch with Gilbert.

Now it was dark and it would have been very difficult for Louis to see clearly into a car driving by so quickly. I thought this seemed strange, so I took up the phone book and looked up his name. I found it right away. I called and asked if this was the same person that we had known in Buffalo. It was! We had been living one block away from him and his new wife, for almost a year, without knowing it.

Then we learned how this had all come about. Gilbert told us that he had met his present wife when he drove his ex-mother-in-law to Toronto to a wedding that she was invited to. At the wedding, he met a girl named Clara. They dated and although she was a Canadian and he was an American they began to see a lot of each other and decided to get married. Gilbert had a daughter from his first marriage and now they had another little girl.

So we became extremely friendly now and saw a lot of each other since we lived only one block away. I became pregnant again and when I had to go to the hospital, I called Clara to take care of our firstborn. I knew I was going to have a boy this time. I just felt it. My point here is that it is almost impossible to imagine that Louis had really seen Gilbert driving by on that dark night and also been able to see the face of a man he thought he knew. It just took a moment for it to change our lives.

Gilbert had developed a pharmaceutical company with his ex-brother-in-law in Manhattan. Now he wanted to start one in Toronto. And he wanted Louis to come to Canada and become a partner in this business. Louis had done his part in the Manhattan Project and now had to find a new job. But he didn't want a job. He wanted his own business. He wanted to be a partner in the business that was going to be established in Toronto.

On the day my son Collin was born, Louis, Gilbert and his partner came into my hospital room. They stood over my bed and said to me, "How would you like to move to Toronto?" I asked, "Where is Toronto?" In those days, and that was 1946, Montreal was the Canadian city that most people knew about. Toronto was not well known. I said, "No, I do not want to move to Toronto."

I said to Louis, "I have moved to Buffalo, I have moved to West Virginia, I have moved to Washington, and I want to live in New York City where my family is. I have not been here in New York for much time since we have been married. So no, I do not want to move again, especially out of the country."

As a rule, Louis never talked very much. He would say what he had to say. If he didn't have anything to say he was quiet. But in this case he talked and talked about moving to Toronto and having a chance to have his own business. He was a good chemical engineer and this was a chance of a lifetime, he said. After much discussion I finally gave in. I decided that if it was that important to him, I would give him a chance. Louis was working with Gilbert setting up the business and I got ready to move to Toronto with a five-month-old baby and a three-year-old girl.

I open up my memory box to a train trip. I remember that awful, awful train trip. I wanted to fly to Toronto, but Louis said "No, I want you to take the train. It's safer." Of course, at that time people were not flying as frequently as they do today. I asked Louis if I needed a passport, a visa, or anything because Canada is a different country. He said "No, you don't need anything. Gilbert and I have been going back and forth and they just wave us through." Of course, they would drive, and at that time, 1946, not many Americans were moving to Canada. More likely more Canadians were trying to move to the USA.

So I did as Louis said. I got on the train for the 12 hour trip. I put the children to bed. I had reserved a room on the train so we had two beds, and I fell asleep myself. About 3 a.m. my son Collin woke up and began to cry. He hardly ever did that. I had a bottle for him but had given it to the porter to put in the refrigerator. I rang for the porter and I asked him to get the bottle. He looked worried. He told me he had put it in the refrigerator in the diner and that part of my train was locked up and he couldn't get it. So I sat up most of the night holding and rocking my son.

When we finally reached the border at Fort Erie, N.Y., Canadian customs officials came on board and asked each person for identification. When they came to me and asked why I was going to Toronto, I very proudly said, "I'm moving to Toronto. My husband is setting up a business there." "Where is your passport?" they asked. I replied that my husband said that I didn't need one. I was told to just wait. They will be back in a few minutes.

When they came back they said," You have to get off the train." I had thought they would be very pleased to know that an American family was moving to Canada and I looked at them and said, "I am not getting off the train. I have a five-month-old baby and a three-year-old girl and it's very hot out there." It was June 15 and the temperature had reached 95° degrees. The sun was burning hot and I refused to leave the train. The other passengers were looking at me because I was holding up the departure of the train.

The customs men took my luggage and threw it on the platform. I had no way to stay on the train without my luggage. They had thrown my luggage on to the platform of the train station that was in Canada and so I was already in Canada. All I had to do was wait for the next train. I was so angry that I thought if I could get to the airport, I would just go back to New York and never leave it.

The next train came and we got seated without any problems, but a 12 hour train trip turned out to be a 24-hour train trip. This was one of the things I will never forget even though it happened almost 70 years ago. I will never ever forget it. That is one of the good things about looking back on your life. You can save the good and the bad and laugh at them.

V

We settled down in a house we had to buy, since there were no apartments available. I open my memory box again to the letter W.

I was in bed in our new house, which I did not like. The house had no personality. One night I was reading the newspaper to catch up on the news before falling asleep. I read a small article about some women starting a lecture series in Michigan. I thought, "I could do that." I turned to tell Louis about the article, but he was already asleep.

The next day I called one of the agents mentioned in the article and told him that I would like to start a lecture series in Toronto. He said, "Yes I can help you." He suggested not only a straight lecture series but to add some travel and adventure lectures to this series. We put together a series of five lectures.

The series would include Lowell Thomas. At that time, Lowell Thomas was a very big name. He was on radio; he travelled and wrote about his experiences. Everybody around the world knew his name. These lecturers would not only appear in person, but they would have full-length films they would narrate in person. It would be a travel-adventure series.

I started to look for a theater where they could perform. There were only two that I could consider. One was Massey Hall, which held 2,750 people, and the other was Eaton Auditorium, created by Lady Eaton. This was a unique theater on top of a department store. It was on the seventh floor and included a foyer and two restaurants. The foyer had comfortable seats and there was a parking lot behind the department store. The theater seated 1,264 people. After speaking to the manager there, I decided that that was the right place for me.

It turned out to be the right decision. I worked hard to develop this series and find subscribers. The timing was exactly right, because the war had ended and people were anxious to start traveling once again. They had not been able to travel during the war. The World Adventure Tours had great success in attracting audiences. I made room for an office in my home, and was able to take care of my children and still keep working.

I had a wonderful time running the World Adventure Tours for 41 years. I met so many interesting people. I got to know the agents who represented the lecturers, and they got to know me. The people who came to perform were excellent speakers since they had to narrate their films, which were silent. They were also excellent cinematographers since they were showing various countries. Some of the lecturers were better than others.

Aside from the series, I sometimes would book special speakers. For example, I booked the Duke of Bedford. I had such fun when he came for the show. I had a call from his agent asking if I wanted to book him and I said sure. People in Toronto and all over Canada were very, very, very interested in anything to do with royalty. Bedford had just written a book called "Silver Spoon." He was just starting on a speaking tour to publicize his new book.

He was very publicity conscious and was in the news quite often, so I thought I would sell out, but tickets were not selling. I had a theater seating 1,264 people. I didn't want to lose money on the Duke. I wondered what I could do and I finally came up with an idea.

I called his home in England and was told he had already left his place, so I picked up the phone and called the editors of the three major newspapers and told them that I had just heard from the Duke and he said he was interested in buying Casa Loma. Casa Loma is probably the only castle in North America and it was being run by a service club in Toronto. Well, the papers came out that evening with enormous headlines announcing that the Duke wanted to buy Casa Loma. The next day Toronto was full of people saying they couldn't let him buy Casa Loma. The newspapers carried stories and cartoons. One of them had Mayor Nathan Phillips standing in front of the castle fighting the Duke who was approaching Casa Loma on horseback, dressed in armor. It was hilarious.

I called his agent and she said that I had better tell him what happened. I didn't know where to reach him so I called the hotel where I had reserved a room for him and said please tell him to call me as soon as he comes in, no matter what time it is. Which he did. When I told him what I had done he laughed. At the press conference I had arranged for him the following morning, everybody in the media came, newspapers, television, radio, everybody was there to meet with the Duke. When one of them asked him how he had heard of Casa Loma. He said, "Some fellow told me about it."

I had a phone call from the president of the service club running Casa Loma and he said, "Of course, we won't let him buy the castle. But as a courtesy, we will let him tour the castle." So that afternoon the Duke and I had a special tour of the castle with television cameras following us throughout the place. They gave him souvenirs of the castle, one of them a pair of salt and pepper shakers and the other, a copy of the castle in the form of a bank. The Duke gave them to me. The papers didn't let the story go. I didn't sell as many tickets as I thought I would, but I had so much fun that I didn't care.

VI

It was the end of summer 1948, and the CNE, the Canadian National Exhibition was about to open. The CNE was the world's longest running annual exhibition and everyone looked forward to it. It had been closed during the war years and now that the war was over, it was free to open it to the public. As a newcomer to Toronto, I had never attended the CNE and I was anxious see what it was like.

I asked friends what it was like, and they said, well it's like going to a country fair. There are lots of buildings near the lakeshore and some of them have animals and there's a building that contains food demonstrations and some of them give out free samples so there are lines of people waiting to get them. There are other buildings that contain commercial merchandise and people just walk around, looking at what there is on display. There are rides for the children.

I asked if there was any entertainment, and I was told that there was a band that would play music. I asked if there were seats for people to sit on while they listened to the music, and I was told that no, there were no seats. I thought about this for quite a while. This was the largest annual fair in the world, and there was no place for people to sit. I couldn't quite understand that, and after thinking about it I decided that I might be able to do something to enhance the CNE.

I called the manager of the fair and made an appointment to see him. I told him I thought I had an idea that might interest him. When I arrived at his office, he greeted me and asked what I had in mind. I told him I had an idea to create a family show with seats, so people could rest after walking around the fair all day. The show would include a comedy act, dancers and music. He said that they had never done anything like that before. I told him perhaps it was time for a change. He asked me if I had anyone in mind for the main headliner? I told him I did. I said I thought I could get Olson and Johnson, who were very big in show business at that time, to agree to come to the CNE. He asked me if I could really get them, and I replied that I was sure I could. I told him I would like to rent the largest building at the CNE for the performances, which we would do in the late afternoon, one show a day.

He asked if I really could get Olson and Johnson and I said I believed that I could. Then he said, "If you can get Olson and Johnson I will let you rent the building." I told him I would like something in writing so that I had an agreement in my hand. He said, "My word is my bond." He put out his hand and shook my hand and said, "Let me know how you make out."

Now the reason I was so sure that I could get Olson and Johnson was because I knew Howard Newman. Howard was an old friend of Louis' from high school days. He had become a Broadway press agent representing Broadway shows. When Howard found out that we had moved to Toronto, he always came to see us when he was coming through with a show that he represented. Because Howard and I had a mutual love for the theater, we became quite close friends.

I knew that Howard was coming through with a show the following week. As usual, he came to see us. I told him about my meeting with the manager of the CNE and my idea to put on a new type of show. I asked him if he knew Olson and Johnson, He said he knew them quite well. He said that if I came to New York, he would introduce me to them.

I made arrangements to fly to New York the following week. I met with Howard and he took me to their show. Obviously, he had told them about me, because in the dialogue during the show, they kept mentioning the name Mrs. Craig and Toronto. So I knew that he had already spoken to them. After the show, Howard took me backstage to meet them in person. They were jolly fellows, constantly making jokes. I liked them. We spoke about them doing the show in Toronto, and I told them what my idea was. They seemed to like it.

However, they said that I would have to speak with their agent before they could do anything more. Their agent worked with the William Morris Agency and I made an appointment to speak with the agent. The Agency was one of the largest in the world, representing many theatrical people as well as others. The agent agreed to meet with me. I was quite young and not experienced in this kind of thing, and I felt that I should not go up there by myself.

I did not know anyone in New York who could go with me, except for my brother-in-law, Joseph Moriber, who was a lawyer. He was tall and had a good personality. We met with the agent, whose name I don't remember right now. He became very enthusiastic as I shared with him what I had in mind. He thought that Olson and Johnson would be ideal for such a show. He complimented me on originating this idea. We had been talking for quite a while and decided that we would meet again the next day and wind up the details.

When we left the agent, Joe and I were very enthusiastic about the reception we had had. Joe agreed to meet with me and the agent the next day. The following day, we met at the agency and started working out the business details, how much Olson and Johnson would get, and other things that we had to finalize. As we were talking the phone rang and it was the manager of the CNE. He said to the agent, Mrs. Craig is no longer representing the CNE. The agent looked at me and I looked at Joe and he looked at me and the agent and we didn't know what to say. The manager said to the agent, "We are taking over this show. We will hire Olson and Johnson and then put the show together ourselves. Mrs. Craig has nothing more to do with the show."

This is the man who said to me, "My word is my bond." I almost became ill. There was nothing I could do. Joe said there was nothing he could do. The agent couldn't do anything except follow orders. I returned to Toronto and spoke to a lawyer. I asked him if I could take out an injunction to prevent the CNE from putting on the show. He said no, unless you have over one million dollars that you can lose. They can sue you if you keep them from putting on the show. They could sue you for close to one million dollars if you don't allow them to put on the show.

The CNE did put on the show, and it was very successful and Olsen and Johnson went over very well. The audience loved having a place to sit and watch a family type show. There were dancers, there was an orchestra and it was so successful that the following year they brought in another big headliner and it continued year after year and made a lot of money for the CNE. I was heartsick over this. It was a good idea. It was my idea. I couldn't go near the CNE grounds for years because of this. I finally managed to sue them and I won the case. But I only got enough money to pay my lawyers.

VII

It would be nice if we could stay young forever. But getting old has its advantages too. Going through life we experience many things. And if we are smart we will retain the memory of these experiences. It helps, when you get to be as old as I am, to remember some of the things that you experienced as you traveled through life. When you're old, people marvel if you remember your name, if you remember where you put your keys, if you remember what you did yesterday, let alone last year or the year before.

I find keeping busy helps me try to outwit Mother Nature. She catches up with us sooner or later. I am still laughing at something that happened over 40 years ago. There was a pharmaceutical convention taking place at a hotel about a four-hour drive from Toronto. It was a two-day, one-night affair and Louis asked me to accompany him. It was a pleasant trip. I brought some books along to read while he was at the convention meetings. In the evening, he wanted to go to bed fairly early and get up early the next morning.

Louis did not like to attend the social affairs of these conventions. It was business for him. We did not have a honeymoon when we were first married, so I thought why not pretend that this was our honeymoon. So I brought along a black silk nightgown with a see-through top. We went to bed fairly early and were reading when we heard some noise in the corridor. It was a band marching down the hall and was very noisy. A lot of the people at this convention liked to live it up at night. There they were striding down the hall, playing their saxophones and trumpets singing and making a lot of noise. It was very, very noisy. Louis did not like that.

As the noise approached our room, he got up and opened the door to tell them to stop. Some of the men looked in and saw me and my black silk nightgown. They tried to get in the room. It was very amusing to see Louis trying to shut the door and the men trying to push the door open so that they could get into the room. Fortunately, Louis succeeded, and pushed the door closed and locked it. He was furious. We went back to reading our books.

When I see older people out on the street and in their wheelchairs or in their scooters, I say to myself, good for them. They are doing things, going places. Many people just wait to do what they want to do. And then they are older and it's too late. I started traveling and never stopped, even to this day, when I'm approaching my hundredth birthday. I remember seeing two women in Banff, Alberta. One tried to help the other. They had a difficult time walking. They could barely make it to their hotel. At that moment, I decided that I would start to travel. I would not wait until I could not walk, or get around easily. Louis said he did not care to travel. He preferred to stay at home.

When our children were at camp in the summer I would have the time to travel. When I was on the stage introducing the artist I had booked for the World Adventure Tours, I had the opportunity to tell over a thousand people that I was planning a trip to a foreign country. I asked the audience if anyone would like to come with me. I usually had a good response.

Louis usually said he wasn't going. I told him not to worry, that I would go with my group. The trips usually lasted ten days, or two weeks. The groups of people consisted of people with the same ideas, since they all wanted to travel and see the places they had seen at the World Adventure Tours series. So bit by bit, we traveled to many places. We always had our own guide and usually our own bus. We took our time. We could stay at a place that interested us as long as we liked, often longer than other groups did. Usually everything went beautifully. I wondered why I had not thought about doing this earlier. Some of the people traveled with me several times, and we became friends. Louis always came on these trips, even though he usually said he wasn't coming.

It wasn't always fun and games though. On one trip, a woman in our group fell down and broke her hip. I had to put her in the hospital and she had to stay there until she recovered. On another trip, a woman came down with pneumonia and had to go to a hospital. But on the whole, it was great fun and a wonderful feeling to be able to travel around the world.

If I tried to travel to those places now, I would have problems. I look at things and think, "I can do it," but when I stand up I find it isn't so easy to do what I think I can do. But I have memories of a lot of the trips I took and I don't regret one.

One of the trips I remember quite well covered Spain, Portugal and Majorca. Some of the people on this trip had traveled with me before, so it was a friendly group. We wound the trip up in Majorca and on our last evening, I asked the group if they wanted to go to a nightclub. They all said they wanted to go. We had a very good time that evening.

Before we went to bed, I told them to make sure that they had their passports and airline tickets ready for our departure the next morning. The next morning I reminded them all again. When we got to the airport, I checked them in and their luggage was put on the plane. We were ready to board. We all had our passports except for one person. This was a woman who had traveled with me before. She told me she could not find her passport, therefore she could not get on the plane. The plane was supposed to depart in a few minutes.

Louis was pulling my arm to get on the plane, but I would not leave her alone. I refused to board the plane. There were several airport police watching us. Louis went over to one of them and tried to bribe him. He was almost arrested. But I would not leave that woman alone in Majorca.

I took her to one side and said to her, "Please try to calm down, I won't leave you. Try to think carefully. When did you see your passport last?" She brightened up and said "I had it last night." "Where did you have it?" I asked. She said "In my evening bag." "And where is your evening bag?" I asked. She said "It's in my luggage." Our group luggage had been loaded much earlier so all the luggage had to be removed in order to reach her suitcase. She opened her luggage and there was her evening bag with her passport. Now she was finally allowed to go on the plane. I'm sure all the other passengers were quite annoyed with us for delaying the flight so long.

VIII

This is a great time to be a senior. It's a brand-new world for those of us who are in their nineties because of the technical wonders that have taken place in the last 10 or 15 years. I remember when I saw my first computer, it frightened me. I didn't know what to do with it. I had been using a typewriter for so many years. I was its master. But the computer became my master. Writing letters is almost obsolete, unless it's a business letter. Everything happens so quickly in the technical world. I can email someone and receive an answer in less than 10 minutes. I find it incredible.

My small great grandchildren know more about the computer now than I do. I no longer worry about having them go near my computer, because they know what I don't know. I wish I could hang around this world for another 20 or 30 years just to see what new things are going to be invented. I just can't imagine what this world will be like.

If I am not hearing so well these days I can listen to stories, biographies, or historical books on audio tape. It's even more interesting when there is a good narrator. As to just picking up a book, it is difficult now, as I can't read well because of my eyesight.

Some people just think it's so unusual and wonderful for me to remember things that I do remember. I am fortunate in having a good memory. I know where I put my keys, I know where my comb and brush are, I remember what I had for dinner yesterday, but I'm not at all sure what I'm going to have tomorrow. When I'm not able to fall asleep for a long time after I go to bed, I reminisce about some of the fun adventures I had during my life.

I remember all too well the time that I booked the Prime Minister of England, Clement Attlee. One day an agent called me and asked if I would be interested in bringing Attlee to Toronto since he was starting on a speaking tour. I said I thought I would be interested and I booked him. I also booked Massey Hall with its 2,750 seats. When I booked him, I made sure that he would come to Toronto a week or two earlier for a press interview. I told myself that Torontonians would just love him, as they loved the Queen.

The night before the interview, to be held the following morning, was a snowy evening and I asked Louis if he would drive me to the airport so that we could meet Attlee and Lady Attlee, and take them to their hotel to prepare for the press interview. At that time, the airport was much smaller than it is today. Since it was so cold and so snowy, we parked in front and I ran in to get the Attlees through immigration.

The interview the following morning was not a great success. Everyone from the media was there, and when they asked questions about the British economy, Attlee said, "I really don't know. I haven't been there for a fortnight."

When I booked him, I was given the choice of several subjects he was to speak on. I chose the one I thought would be best for us. But he seemed to be giving only one talk wherever he spoke, whether it was for clubs, universities or individual people like me who had booked him.

The reviews on his speech were not favorable. I managed to get the name of someone who had booked him, and I was told that it was just not good. I began to have doubts about this booking. I called his agent and told him that ticket sales were very bad. I said that Attlee seemed to be speaking on only one subject. I wondered if he was going to stick to the same subject he was giving wherever he went.

The agent said, "Would you feel better if I asked him to call you and tell you that he was going to speak on that other subject?" I said, "Yes, I would feel better if I knew that he was going to talk on the subject I had selected." This was about two weeks before he was to come to Toronto. I had already called the mayor and said that I had booked a Prime Minister of England and thought we should do something for him. The mayor agreed with me and said he would give a dinner for Attlee. He told me to make out a list of guests.

As time progressed, the reviews of Attlee's speeches were getting worse and worse. I didn't know what to do. I told the manager at Massey Hall that I wanted to cancel Attlee. He said he would not charge me although he had been holding the date. He said, "If I were in your place, I would cancel." I called my lawyer, who also advised me to cancel. He told me the agency could make me pay the full fee, but they might not choose to come to Canada to sue me. He said, "If you allow him to come to speak, you will have to pay his fee in full. The agency may require you to pay if you cancel, but on the other hand, they may not want to go through all the legalities of it. If I were you, I would cancel."

I don't know how the press picked up the news that I had canceled a Prime Minister of England, but it was in all the papers all over the world. My phone never stopped ringing. My sister in New York saw the story on the front page of the New York Times. The mayor called me and said, "What have you done to my dinner?" I told him I hadn't done anything to his dinner and he could still have it if he wanted to.

The next day Attlee called me and asked, "Can I still come to the dinner?" I told him it was up to him, I was out of the picture. But the press never stopped calling me. The day of the dinner the mayor called me and said, "I want you to go to the airport to pick up the Attlees who are arriving today for the dinner." I told him that I was not responsible for the Attlees anymore. "It's your dinner." The mayor said, "You are responsible for this. I have no one else to go to meet them and I want you to do it," and he hung up the phone. I asked Louis if he would drive me to the airport. He said he couldn't. We had a new car, a lovely Lincoln Continental, and I had only driven it a few times.

I didn't want to go alone because I knew reporters and photographers would be there to greet the Attlees. I knew if they saw me with them it would be quite a story so I called the British Trade Commissioner and asked him if he would go with me. He said he would come and his wife would come along with us. He added that his car was too small for five people so I said we would use my car.

Before I left for the trip I asked Louis if there was enough gas in the car. He said there was. But when I looked at the gauge I could see it was on E for empty. But Louis said there was still plenty of gas. I left to pick up the trade commissioner and his wife and we drove to the airport. I parked in front and told the trade commissioner that I would wait there while he and his wife went in to get the Attlees. I could see reporters were there to take pictures of the Attlees and I did not want them to find me, so I hid in a corner near the front door.

Finally when the Attlees came out, I joined them and went to get into the car. But there was no car. I found out that it had been towed away. There were piles of snow all over the place. I had no boots on. I had to retrieve the car going through all the snow. I drove it to the front of the airport and the reporters watched as the trade commissioner and his wife and the Attlees got in the car. Of course, that made a story that the car had been towed away. Louis didn't think it was very funny.

When we were on our way back, the trade commissioner suggested that we stop off at his house for some tea. Everyone thought this was a great idea, so we did just that. I was anxious to get them to their hotel. I had to get back home and get ready for the dinner because the mayor had insisted that I attend. After the tea and a little more conversation, the commissioner offered us a second cup of tea. I told them "We don't have time for that, I have to get them to their hotel." So I hustled the Attlees into the car.

Now for the first time I'm alone with the Attlees in the backseat and I'm in the driver's seat. It was an awkward time for me. I knew that they were unhappy over the fact that I had canceled him. To make conversation I told Lady Attlee that we had some very fine shops that she might like to visit. She said very briskly, "We don't have much of that kind of money to go shopping." I was very happy when we arrived at the Royal York Hotel.

Alone in my car I started for home. On a very busy intersection in the city, about 5 o'clock in the afternoon, in the middle of the street the car stalled. I couldn't start it and finally got another car to push me over to the side. No matter what I did, I could not start the car. I suspected that it was out of gas. I called Louis and told him what had happened. I said it was out of gas and that I should have it towed away. Louis told me it was not out of gas. He told me to go back and try to start it again. So I did, but I could not start the car. I called him again. He said he would come right down using my little car. I was worried because I had very little time before the dinner was to start. I had to change for the dinner and feed the children before leaving. There was not much time for all that.

Louis came and he tried to make the car start but he couldn't do it. In the end, we had to have the car towed away. And we went back home. While I was dressing the phone rang. It was the mayor's secretary telling me to hurry down, that they were delaying the dinner until we got there. Well, we got to the dinner, which was a good one. Then Attlee got up and made a speech. He was funny. I thought to myself that if he had spoken that way on his tour he would have had wonderful reviews and I never would have canceled him. At the end of the day, the Attlees at least had their dinner. The mayor had his dinner. And it didn't cost me the enormous fee I would have had to pay.

IX

Being a senior has its good parts and its bad parts. I don't like having to depend on people to do certain things for me. I don't like what the years have done to me. I have been independent all my life. I would love to go skipping down that road of life forever. My hearing has been cut in half. My eyesight is not good. But I consider myself very fortunate to be able to do whatever I can do for myself as I approach my hundredth birthday. I have stopped going to the theater because it's too uncomfortable for me to sit in the seat for such a long time. I have given up going to concerts and lectures for the same reason. I can watch some television programs and, of course, I can watch the news.

The news is not very good, and I sometimes think I would be better off if I didn't watch those programs. I don't know why people don't want more peace. I can't understand why there is so much fighting, and

I think too many people have access to too many guns.

I was born at the end of the First World War. I grew up during the Great Depression, which was not a great time for most people. Even with a bad economy we didn't worry about terrorists, or riots in the streets, or guns in so many peoples' hands. If we could stop the sales of guns to anybody and everybody, we could have a better world. Many politicians are interested in their own political party, never mind what the results are for the public. I have seen during my lifetime good and bad. There were not so many wars. People were kinder to each other but science has made great strides. Cancer will be cured, I am sure. The future looks very wonderful to me.

Creating the World Adventure Tours shows opened a new world to me. I began to meet many interesting people, sometimes through the performers, and sometimes the performers themselves. I met the Grand Duchess Olga through a performer I brought to Toronto, who became a good friend to me and my husband. His name was Nicol Smith, a very interesting person, the son of Susie Smith who was famous in Hollywood as a columnist. Nicol was a favorite of my audiences. He knew everybody all over the world. And if he didn't know them personally, he knew someone who knew them.

One day when he came to Toronto to do a show for me, he told me that he was having a dinner party for the Grand Duchess Olga, and invited my husband and me to attend. Now Olga hardly ever went out. The evening of the dinner party the weather was cold, rainy, and windy. I said to Louis that I didn't think Olga would go out in that kind of weather since she rarely went out at all. But we had told Nicol that we would come to his dinner party. So we went.

When we got to his hotel suite, we found that Olga did come out, even though the weather was so bad. We had a lot of fun that night, having drinks and dinner. About two months later I received an invitation in the mail from Olga, inviting me to the wedding of her son, Prince Kulikowski. I asked Louis to come with me, but he refused. So I asked a friend to come instead.

When we arrived at the church, we found a number of guests already there. But there were no seats. There were no seats for anyone. Olga stood by herself on a little round rug near the altar. We stood with the other guests. Shortly after, the bride and groom came out with six men following them, three men behind the bride and three men behind the groom. The men were there to hold crowns over the heads of the couple. If the first man in the line felt his arm tremble, he would pass the crown to the second man. That way the crown would never fall.

The couple approached the altar and the ceremony began. Finally the bride and groom walked around three times and the ceremony was over. It had taken over an hour. Olga and the guests had been standing all this time. There was no sign of a reception, or of any food or drinks, so we all went home. I sent the prince and his wife a gift. I was sorry to learn that they were divorced two years later.

I guess the highlight of the World Adventure Tours was when I brought Sir Edmund Hillary and his crew to Toronto and Montreal. Louis never knew who I was bringing to do the shows, but when he found out that I had booked Hillary he was very excited. Hillary, of course, was the most famous man in the world at that time. He had climbed to the top of Mt. Everest. He was the first man to ever attempt and complete the climb to the top of Mt. Everest. Now Hillary was on a tour to raise money for the Sherpa mountain guides to be able to open schools to educate their children. I booked Massey Hall for his performance. The place was sold out as soon as it was announced that Hillary and his crew were coming to Toronto.

I had not realized how many people were interested in mountain climbing nor did I know that there were various types of mountain climbers and that they have clubs. The head of one of the clubs phoned and asked me if they could host a lunch for Hillary and his crew at the University of Toronto. Of course I agreed to that. I arranged a press conference for Hillary and then took him to meet top government officials. They did not seem as enthusiastic as I thought they would be. That night after the show, the people went wild. As we came out of the stage door we found that crowds had gathered. One man reached out and touched Hillary's shoulder and cried, "I touched him." Then we had to leave for Union Station to take the train to Montreal, where he would face another audience.

Montreal was a different scene altogether. We were invited to the mayor's office and had a police escort take us there. The mayor of Montreal was excited to meet Sir Edmund Hillary. Lady Hillary arrived and joined us for the little party that the mayor gave us, serving wine and some food. It was totally different than the reception Hillary had in Toronto. I was able to use two large auditoriums, seating over 3,500 people. Again the show was all sold out. It was so thrilling to feel the excitement of the crowds. Everybody went wild. It was a night to remember.

I wanted to talk about it, but Louis wanted to go back to the hotel and go to bed. I just wanted to sit down over a drink or something just to talk about it. But he didn't feel like it. So we settled by having a fruit cup at a nearby drug store. The next morning, a police officer knocked at the door of my hotel room and I was presented with six copies of the pictures that had been taken of all of us at the mayor's office the night before.

Running the World Adventure Tours was almost a full time job. It took quite a bit of work to fill a theater several times a week. The audience never knew when things were going wrong back stage. The theater was a union house. The crew back stage belonged to a union. The projectionist was a union man. We had to take whoever they sent. They kept sending us Laurence. The problem was that Laurence had faulty eye sight, and could barely see the screen. The show usually consisted of the narrator live on the stage and his film behind him. The film and the narration had to go together. The performers used 16mm film. Commercial theaters used 35 mm film that does not have to be adjusted all the time. But 16 mm has to be adjusted all the time.

Laurence didn't seem to care about that. He didn't bother about the focus at all. Calling up to the projection booth proved to be useless. I wanted my audiences to have a good show. I protested to the union. But they kept sending Laurence. It was a no win situation. I finally solved the dilemma by hiring another projectionist who was not a union man to sit with Laurence and tell him when the film needed focusing. This added to the cost of the production, but it certainly helped the performance and I think the audience appreciated it.

X

Memories! So many memories! I well remember attending a conference and I won a door prize there. The door prize consisted of my receiving a dozen roses once a month for a year. You can imagine the thrill of opening my door on a blustery January day to find a delivery man with a dozen roses. Actually it was a baker's dozen. There were 13 roses, which I received once a month. What a door prize it was.

Another great thrill was a birthday gift I received from Louis. He didn't know what to give me. I had seen an ad that an excellent beauty salon was having a sale on massages. Up to this point, I had never had a massage. The cost was very low for a place like that, five massages for 50 dollars, 10 dollars a massage. So I asked him if I could have that for my birthday gift. Of course he said yes and we ordered them. When it was a very miserable day I would go down and have a massage. So many years later, I can even now visualize the feeling that I had. I was very choosy about the day I would have the massage since there were only five in this package. I found it so great when I had it. That was a wonderful gift.

I remember when Louis and I were in Lisbon, Portugal. This was part of a trip we were on. We had stopped off in Lisbon for Louis to meet with some doctors with whom he was doing business. They invited us to have dinner with them at their country club. I had expected them to have their wives with them, but they didn't. I asked if their wives were coming later. They said no. They said wives did not go out at night.

After dinner the entertainment started, featuring a fado singer. The fado music was a kind of blues song. A woman came out dressed in black, with a shawl over her shoulders, and she started to sing that fado music. So many bad things were happening to her. Her husband was unfaithful, her children were terrible, her mother scolded her. Whatever was bad was happening to her.

This was Fado music and I found it very interesting. I thought I would write a little script for radio featuring Fado music. Since I had never heard of Fado, I thought there might be many people like me who didn't know that kind of music. So I bought a Fado record and wrote a script and brought it down to the Canadian Broadcasting Corporation.

Now I had never written for radio and I really didn't know how to go about it. I did what I thought I should do, and I was ecstatic when they bought it immediately and told me it would be broadcast coast to coast across Canada. They didn't change a word that I had written. The night it was on Louis was out and I sat with my mother-in-law who had been visiting us. When the program was over, I expected her to say it was good, it was bad. I wanted her to say something. She did. All she said was, "Did they pay you for it?"

Yes, I was paid. Because I had been successful in selling my very first radio script, I decided to do another. I sold that one too. Then I bought the type of tape recorder that the Canadian Broadcasting Corporation wanted us to use and took it with me whenever I traveled. I did interviews with all sorts of people, whether they were ordinary folk or famous. I wrote scripts about places I visited, and inserted interviews in the scripts. I became very adept at using the tape recorder, which had two reels on it. One reel had a tape, which would wind itself onto the other reel. I taught myself to cut the tape, eliminate a wrong word, and put the tape together again so it flowed nicely along. Finally, I got my own radio show on another station. It was a weekly show and I loved doing it.

XI

Louis and I were in Rome. We were to leave for home the following day, but I suddenly felt that there was something I wanted to do before we left. I wanted to interview Elizabeth Taylor who was starring in the movie, Cleopatra. Of course I had my trusty tape recorder with me because in those days I never traveled without it. I was going to call a cab to take me to the film studio, and I asked Louis if he would like to come with me. He said the idea was ridiculous. He said, "You don't just walk in and say you want to interview Elizabeth Taylor. You have to make plans weeks in advance." I said, "I would take a chance." I proceeded to call a cab.

Of course, Louis came with me. We drove to the outskirts of Rome where the film studio was located. Naturally, there was a guard house at the entrance and we were supposed to stop. But I suddenly discovered that I could speak Italian. I said to the driver, "Avanti." He did.

We drove straight through. We saw a number of extras sitting around in their costumes. I don't know how I knew where the studio Elizabeth Taylor was working in was located, but I just felt that I did know and I stopped the cab outside this particular studio. We paid the driver and climbed the steps to the door. I put my hand on the knob of the door but saw a red light flashing. I knew that meant they were filming. And I knew also that if I opened the door, I would destroy everything they were doing at that moment.

So we waited, and as we stood there a woman came running up and she was furious. She said, "What are you doing here?" I said, "I want to interview Elizabeth Taylor for the Canadian Broadcasting Corporation." She told me that would be arranged through the publicity office. She added, "Come back to the publicity office and we will see when we can fit you in." Well, we were quite a distance from the publicity office, which was located near the entrance. I told her we did not have a car and it was too far to walk. She said, "I will send a car for you." And she did.

When we arrived at the publicity office, I was given a huge press kit and saw lots of photos from the film Elizabeth Taylor and Richard Burton were making together. There were a lot of rumors around Rome about their romance. It was hot stuff. The woman asked me if I would like to meet Taylor's understudy. Of course, I wanted to. She was very beautiful. She looked just like Elizabeth Taylor. Then the press woman said, "We can arrange for you to do an interview in two weeks." I told her we were leaving Rome the next day. She said she would let us tour one of the sets if we wanted to. I was not to interview the understudy, and Louis, who was carrying a camera, was told that he was not to take pictures. We were escorted out to the set.

I had a long talk with the understudy and Louis took pictures of the set. It was enormous. It was an outdoor set on a field as big as a football field. There was a huge throne on the ground. It was thrilling to see. I know it was a crazy thing to do, but it was a fun thing and I'm glad we did it.

From time to time, I took several courses at the University of Toronto. Then I heard about the adult education school at Ryerson College, now Ryerson University. It was easier for me to attend Ryerson, and I liked the courses they had. Then I learned about their Act II Studio, which had been started about two years earlier. I immediately joined the then small group. I auditioned for parts in plays and was cast in some of them. It was fun working with groups of people who enjoyed the theater as much as I did.

Since I liked writing radio scripts, I thought I would try to write a play. I don't know where I got the idea to write about a woman who was told she had only six months to live. She decides that she wants to be buried in a pyramid. When her friends learn about this, they help her try to find a proper place to build a pyramid.

The play was a comedy. Act II Studio liked it and rented a theater where it ran for a week. That started another career for me. I have since written seven more plays, all of them, but one, staged and performed.

XII

When I was around fourteen or fifteen years old, I would delight in going to concerts that the Dennis Shawn Dancers performed. Ruth St. Denis and Ted Shawn had combined their dancers to form the Dennis Shawn Dancers. I loved watching them. They did modern ballet and it was so interesting, I was entranced by them.

Many years later, after I had moved to Toronto, I heard that Ted Shawn was touring, giving a lecture and demonstrating some of his dance steps. I thought this was an opportunity to see him again. Since Toronto was so full of ballet lovers, I was sure that people would turn out to watch him and listen to his lecture.

I rented the 2,756 seat Massey Hall because I was sure every ballet lover would want to get in. I didn't even bother to do the usual press releases I generally did before the shows I presented. Ted Shawn arrived on the day of the concert with his valet. He asked Louis if he would please come backstage to help Shawn change costumes. I was mortified to find that only one third of the seats had been sold for the performance. It wasn't so much that I was taking a huge loss, but the fact that Shawn was not going to appear before a full house.

The performance was great. I really enjoyed it, despite my disappointment. Of course, Ted Shawn was going to get his full fee. That didn't depend on whether there was only one person in the audience, or if it was sold out. Louis and I took Ted Shawn and his valet out for dinner and we talked of many things. He told us that he was planning to open a new theater called Jacob's Pillow, in the same neighborhood as the famous Tanglewood Music Center.

The next year we were on a motor trip and we were not far from Tanglewood and Jacob's Pillow. We went to Jacob's Pillow and Ted Shawn welcomed us warmly, inviting us to a performance which was just about to start.

I learned a great lesson when I booked Ted Shawn. I had assumed that I would sell out. One should never assume in show business, or in any business, when it comes to that. I thought the Toronto ballet lovers would flock to our show. The ballet lovers wanted pure and simple dance. Ted Shawn's dancers performed a more sophisticated type of dance, which apparently they did not want. I never again made the mistake of assuming what was going to happen. But we did have a lot of laughs with Ted Shawn. We did enjoy having dinner with Ted and his valet. Louis told me later that while he was helping the valet dress Shawn, he noticed that even though Shawn was in his 60's his body was that of a man in his 40's.

XIII

I remember meeting and chatting with Whoopi Goldberg in the ladies room at the Russian Tea Room in Manhattan. I remember driving Dorothy Lamour to a press luncheon. She was practically crying on my shoulder because she was not getting any work in films any more. She complained that Bing Crosby and Bob Hope were getting work all the time and they were older than she was.

Tony Bennet has an excellent voice and I like listening to him. He enjoys painting as well as singing, and he had an art showing in Palm Beach. We were invited to the opening. Louis and I looked at the paintings and when we sat down Tony came over to greet us. Louis said to him, "I can't sing as well as you do but I can paint as well as you do." I was horrified to hear that, and Tony's jaw dropped and he stared at Louis and walked away. Louis didn't think he had done anything wrong, but I thought we better leave the art show at once.

It was a pleasure meeting Steve Allen and his wife Jayne Meadows when we were on a cruise ship. They had come aboard for the duration of two ports to entertain the passengers. We were in the indoor dining room. We were the only passengers in the room because Louis did not like eating out on deck. Suddenly we saw Steve Allen and his wife walk in. I recognized them at once. They were seated at the very next table to us, so I couldn't avoid looking at them. I had always admired his evening shows. When we finally got up to leave we had to pass their table. It would have been rude not say anything, so I welcomed them on board.

I told Steve I had always enjoyed his shows. Then I told him I had read that he used several tape recorders and did he ever get them mixed up. He stood up, took out a recorder from his pocket, and showed it to me. He said he always carried at least one with him. I asked how his secretary knew which one to use. Steve said she could always figure it out. I attended their shows and evening performances on board the ship and, as usual, he was delightful.

How can I forget swimming in a pool full of freshly cut gardenias? We were in a small town in Mexico. The hotel where we were staying had a swimming pool and every morning the staff would cut a number of gardenias and conduct a ceremony at the edge of the pool and put in the gardenias. The guests could enter the pool, if they liked. It was delightful to swim with the gardenias tickling your nose and the fragrance of the flowers overwhelming your entire body. At the end of the day, the gardenias would be gathered together by the staff as they held another ceremony. Then they would clean the pool. I can't smell a gardenia without thinking about that wonderful time swimming among the flowers.

I well remember seeing the Shah of Persia, as Iran was then called. This was in Majorca, where he had his yacht moored in the water outside our hotel. Our room had a balcony, which overlooked the water. At night we could see the lights on the Shah's yacht. One morning we were on our balcony when we saw the Shah and his wife and their dog climb into a small motor boat. They were headed straight to our hotel. His wife was beautiful. She was his first wife, and he loved her. But she was unable to produce an heir for him, so he had to divorce her, even though he loved her.

XIV

I grew up in a very interesting period. It's true, there was the Depression and the Second World War, but interesting things were starting to develop. For one thing, women had to go to work during the war. They did not want to just stay home. Having replaced the men, and seen what it was like to work outside the home with other people, they did not want to simply remain at home any more. They wanted to earn a salary, and they liked working with other people.

I almost blush when I think of the exquisite pangs of emotion I had when I was 15 or 16. I suppose many teenagers go through this stage of life. I would be alone in my parents' apartment listening to the radio, playing one of my favorite songs, watching the sunset. What would my future be? I was a woman of the world. I could do anything I wanted to do. I would meet the man of my dreams. At that moment, it felt great to be a teenager.

I remember my first pair of silk stockings. They were silk because rayon had not been invented yet. I was given the silk stockings because we were all getting dressed up to celebrate my grandparents' Golden anniversary. I cherished those stockings, and wore them only when I was going out on a special occasion, just something special. If I got a run in them, I repaired them very carefully.

So many things happened while I was still a small child. The first time I ever saw a zipper was when I was nine years old and my sister gave me a birthday present of a pencil case with a zipper. I was thrilled with it. We didn't have zippers on clothing then. Men's trousers had only buttons, no zippers. At the beach men had to wear bathing suits, not just trunks. Women then had to wear full-length bathing suits. No one had ever heard of a bikini. There was no such thing as teenage-size clothes. We only had small adult sizes.

There were no traffic lights, and policemen stood on busy streets and directed traffic by hand. Sometimes it almost looked as if they pointed their bodies in one direction or another, as though they were dancing.

Our desks at school had little inkwells on top. No one ever thought there would be such a thing as email then. Personal letters are seldom written now.

You can send a message and get an answer in your email in less than 10 minutes.

Travel has changed so much. I well remember vividly when one of my aunts and her husband took their first trip to Europe. The whole family was excited for them. When they returned, everybody got together to hear their stories of what they had seen in Paris and London. It was a big deal for them to travel overseas. Air traffic was not heavy and it was a pleasure to fly then.

I grew up in a very nice apartment building in Manhattan. The building had an elevator and I remember the elevator operator very well. His name was Ralph. But many buildings then did not have elevators. They were called walk-ups and that's what people did. They walked up. There was no such thing as a condominium. You rented an apartment and paid your rent every month. Twice when we lived in Manhattan, Louis and I put our furniture in storage in the spring and rented a small place at the seashore. It was easy to find an apartment to rent when we came back to the city in the fall.

Children at school today are adept at using computers, but I must confess that even though I have had several computers, I am still a little confused by them. A three-year-old child could probably use one better than I know how to use them.

The technical world has exploded to such an extent that I find amazing. My hearing is not as good as I would like it to be and so I am now using audio tapes. I would rather read the book in its original form, but I cannot read well because of my eyesight. So I am grateful for the audio tapes, particularly if they have a good narrator. If the story is well written and the narrator is good, I am elated.

When we used to go shopping for food, the grocer would add up your purchases on the back of a brown paper bag, put the items in the bag and you would then hand him cash. He would put the money in a drawer, which was divided into compartments for such things. Then along came cash registers. That was great. The salesperson rang up your purchases on the cash register and you would pay in cash. Then came computers and sometimes the computers didn't work. So you couldn't take your purchases. You had to wait until the computer worked again. I'm not sure that is progress.

The United States had television before we did in Canada. It was always a delight when we visited my parents and turned on their television set. Some people turned their sets on before the program was scheduled to start. There was a pattern on the screen when the set was turned on. So people would simply sit and look at the pattern on the screen until the program started. As I recall, there were three networks. One of them decided to put on a program of various acts. They needed someone to host the program. They couldn't find anyone who was interested in the job.

Ed Sullivan, who was a sports writer on a daily newspaper, volunteered to host the program. It turned out to be like a vaudeville show. I was delighted because I had loved vaudeville. Sullivan knew nothing about television. But at that time, hardly anyone knew very much about it. Everyone would watch the Sullivan program every Sunday night and talk about it later. Tuesday night became Milton Berle night, and when we were able, we bought a TV set and watched those programs in our own home. Television has come a long way since then. We have more choices now.

Today we don't have to go to a store to buy something if we don't want to. We can shop online. We can buy books, clothing, almost anything. Very often the price for the item is much less than a retail store would charge. In many ways, life is easier today, but in many ways it is more difficult, especially for older people who cannot adjust to this new world and its technical advances. Who would ever imagine that we could land a man on the moon! Who could imagine such a thing as an iPhone, enabling one to take pictures, read stories, play games.

I don't have an iPhone. I think I'm probably one of the few people who do not own an iPhone. We all take for granted these advances we have made. Some of them have been very helpful. For example, we now have an abundance of plastic bags, which we use for various purposes. How did we ever live without plastic bags? We use them for everything. I'm sure there are many other things that we use in our everyday life.

I like the idea of having air conditioning. It certainly helps when the temperature is too high for comfort. I can recall summers in New York. Sometimes it was so hot we couldn't sleep, so our family would go down to the beach with blankets and spend the night there.

One of the most important inventions that we have is the refrigerator. I well recall the iceman coming into our apartment with ice to put in our icebox. Some people did not even have ice boxes. They used their fire escapes to keep food in good condition. Who can say what we will have 25 or 50 years from now? I know I won't be around but my grandchildren and my great-grandchildren will.

XV

The very last group I escorted abroad was in 1979. China had just opened its borders to foreigners and, as tourists, we were anxious to see what it was like. I gathered together a small group of people to visit China and Egypt. We went first to Egypt and the highlight of the trip, at least for me, was the night we spent sitting on the desert sand. Chairs had been placed before the three pyramids. It was an enchanting evening. There were no lights except for the stars and the moon. Our chairs were directly in front of the pyramids. Suddenly a light shone on one of them. The pyramid spoke and a light would shine on it. What a wonderful evening that was.

On a previous visit to Cairo I had driven with my group from Alexandria, where our ship was moored. After a great dinner and show at the hotel we returned to Alexandria in darkness. The bus driver turned off his headlights, no one in the bus spoke. It was eerie. We drove in silence with no lights. We saw no other cars and no one but a few Berber tribespeople along the way. But this past evening was different. The sound and light performance at the pyramids was something I will never forget.

We were a small group so we had to join another group in order to enter China. We joined the other group in Hong Kong and were now 20 people, which is what the Chinese expected us to have. In Hong Kong, we boarded a train which took us into China. The train was extremely clean. We came to a bridge and the train stopped. We were ushered out onto a platform where there were soldiers who lined us up one by one. There was a small hut and we entered, one by one. We were questioned by a soldier. He wanted to know how much money we were bringing with us. After a few more questions we returned to the train and the train crossed the bridge.

Our group was very lucky because we were heading for what was then Peking and is now called Beijing. We were taken to the best hotel there but it was not very grand. It was very old and there were roaches in the closets. But it was in a great section of the city and we were able to walk around and observe the people. Hardly anyone had a car. Only the VIPs were able to drive around in their cars. Everyone else had a bicycle. The people would lock their bicycles up so no one else could take them.

In 1979, you were told where you could go in China, not where you wanted to go, not what you wanted to see. Chairman Mao had recently died and Hua was the new chairman but Mao's picture was everywhere. Mao's body was laid in a clear glass coffin in Tiananmen Square. We were taken there to see him. Since we were foreigners, we did not have to stand on line to see him. Chinese people were driven in from all over the country to view the coffin. When we came on the scene, the line was halted and we were taken past the coffin without waiting. We were warned not to say a word while we were on line and while we were passing the coffin. The coffin was enhanced by pale lavender lights. It was a very impressive sight with so many soldiers guarding it.

Changes were on the way in China. On a return visit several years later, we had lunch in a really grand hotel, which was glittering with a gold and ebony motif. But on this visit, things were already beginning to change. Before the people could not run their own businesses, but now they could. But they had nothing new to sell and we saw numerous people standing with piles of cabbages that they hoped to sell. They had nothing else.

Walking around Peking, as it was then, we saw huge billboard type of structures so people could write some of their likes and dislikes. We were taken to a hospital where people were operated on without anesthetics. They were given acupuncture and they seemed quite happy. Just as we were interested in the Chinese, they were interested in us. They had not seen many people like us. We were an unfamiliar race to them.

I remember going into a shop to buy some trinkets. I really wanted a Mao's cap. While bending over a counter, I looked up and saw a crowd of Chinese people staring at me. I was as strange to them as they were to me. I asked our Chinese guide whether he wanted to be a guide and I was told no. He wanted to be a teacher. But he was told that he would be a guide. He had no control over his future.

One day we were taken by train to see the Great Wall. It happened to be a very windy day. The road stretched for many miles but the wind made it difficult to walk. There was a little shelter where there was a heater. My hands were frozen. I had not thought to bring gloves. This was, I believe, the beginning of November. So I walked a bit and ran back to the shelter to warm my hands. Then I walked a bit more and ran back to the shelter again. I was mortified to find graffiti on the sides of the Great Wall. I can't imagine anyone trying to destroy such a historical monument as the Great Wall.

Could I ever forget Tangiers, the snake charmer on the street, the snake responding to his commands? How could I ever forget the Medina in Fez in Morocco? This was the longest Medina in the world, a long narrow road where I walked in front of a donkey who would have pushed me out of the way if I hadn't walked faster. I remember the tradesmen with their wares, the people in native dress. It was very exotic.

But life goes on. Or does it? I think the worst day in my life was the day my mother died when she was sitting in an airplane next to my father. They were going from New York to Florida, where they were going spend several months of the winter. Her sisters were waiting for her at the airport in Florida. And then she suddenly died and the flight was aborted. The second worst day of my life was when I lost my right eye due to the incompetence of the surgeon who operated on me.

I think the happiest day of my life was the day my sister was married. On the same day, my first grandson was born. What great news that was. Louis and I went first to the hospital to see our new grandson and then we flew to New York to attend my sister's wedding. It was her first and only time she married. She was 62 years old.

From then on Louis and I did our traveling mostly on cruise ships. We had seen so much of the world. He had never been as keen on travel as I was, so when we were on a cruise and reached port he would often stay on board ship and I would go ashore.

XVI

When I turned 95, my daughter Robin decided to make a documentary about some of the things I have done in my life. The Public Broadcasting System PBS liked it and decided to run it on 400 of their stations. They had a two year contract and when it ended they asked if they could have another three year contract. The reviews were quite good, and some of the stations ran the film several times. It was called, "Stella is 95".

Around that time, I decided to establish an award program for playwrights for the Act II Studio. I had enjoyed writing plays for the Act II Studio. They had produced some of my plays and I wanted to thank them for it. I also hoped that the Stella Award would attract more writers, and it certainly did.

On my 99th birthday my family honored me by adding my name to the Act II Studio and it will remain the Estelle Craig Act II Studio as long as

Ryerson University exists. I am one lucky person to have such a devoted family.

Mother Nature is a funny lady. She gives and she takes. I have lost inches in height. My hearing has been affected and my sight has diminished. I have asked a number of people if they would like to do it all over again and most of them have said, "Oh no. I've had enough." I know I have made many mistakes during my life. I wish I could retract them. But I find life very exciting even though I will soon be 100 years old. I would do it again in a flash if I could. Therefore I have made up a list of rules, which help make living great.

1) Keep busy.

2) If you don't remember the name of someone you know that you know, just call them "honey".

3) If you don't have a hobby, get one.

4) It's easier to smile than to frown, so smile, darn you, smile.

5) If you want to eat ice cream for breakfast, you're allowed to do it.

6) 6) People are not interested in your aches and pains. So don't tell them.

7) 7) If you want to get rid of your wrinkles, take off your glasses when you look in the mirror.

8) You do not have to eat any food you don't like.

9) Take advantage of the new inventions that this decade has given us. Don't be afraid to try them.

10) Keep busy.

I have had a very interesting and a very exciting life. I have three great children, numerous grandchildren, and many great-grandchildren. There are a number of things I would have changed in my life but how can one know what the best choice is until it's over? Rosalind Russell said in the film "Auntie Mame", "Life is a banquet and some poor souls out there are starving to death." I have dined well at the banquet. I am not hungry at all.

About the Author

Stroll down memory lane with Estelle Craig at the age of 100, as she recalls her childhood, life as a new bride, a columnist, an impresario, a radio host and a playwright.

Travel around the world, and meet celebrities.

Find out how it can be fun to be a senior.